This Is Not a Letter
and Other Poems

THIS IS NOT A LETTER
AND OTHER POEMS

BY
KAY BOYLE

Sun & Moon Press
Los Angeles

Copyright © Kay Boyle, 1985
Some of the poems in this collection appeared previously in
The Malahat Review (Canada), *Pearl* (Sweden), *Rolling Stock,*
Willow Springs Magazine, and *Wind.*
Cover: Page I from the Japanese volume *Iseshu*
Design: Katie Messborn
Publication of this book was made possible, in part, by a
grant from the National Endowment for the Arts and contributions
to the Contemporary Arts Educational Project, Inc.

Library of Congress Cataloging-in-Publication Data

Boyle, Kay, 1902-
    This is not a letter and other poems.

    I. Title.
PS3503.09357T538 1985   811'.52   85-20778
ISBN 0-940650-61-4
ISBN 0-940650-62-2 (signed)

FIRST EDITION

10   9   8   7   6   5   4   3   2   1

Sun & Moon Press
6363 Wilshire Blvd. Suite 115
Los Angeles, California 90048

Contents

for Grace Paley

Excerpts from
A Poem for Samuel Beckett

I'll not discuss death with you by any name, however
    gently, soberly, you ask.
When the spectacle of it comes downstage, well off-
    center, "white hair,
White nightgown, white socks," let humor lead the
    onslaught decked out
In coat-of-mail, broadsword or flash-light in gaunlet,
    no matter which.
Buckle on uproarious wit, lower the visor so that no
    convulsed member of the audience
Glimpse the whitening eye or lip a-quiver with palsy.
    Then are we authorized to dance,
Hand in clanking hand (though two continents, one
    ocean intervene); suffered to sing,
But not with the voice of mourning dove in the tearful
    willow grieving,

"*Seul, pas seul. Seul, pas seul*," but between strophes
    preening, grooming,
The few remaining feathers of our iridescence, lovely
    they were—but stop the music!
No past tense permitted either here or there.

Maybe, maybe, I say, Krapp speaks (not spoke) for all
    eternity, his tape my tape as well,
And the voice that mysteriously whispers now off-stage
    asking "what is required of me
That I am tormented thus . . ."? Or saying (whisper-
    ing still) that the humming-bird
Is "known as the passing moment . . . it comes in
    from the right" to fly
In a "lightning semi-circle deasil," then comes a shim-
    mering respite, "then the next
Then then . . ." O, words akin to flying bird hum to
    the tongue at closing time
When drink completes its circle, and you neither
    helping nor hindering me,
Nor lending me your arm as I flounder through the
    door, chasing the last bus

Wending its way up Grafton in the summer dark.
  Maybe, maybe, I say,
It's the contour of the island that is to blame, the shape
  of a harp enough
To have caused all the trouble, but no answer's forth-
  coming; for what country
In its right mind, I go on with it, would choose a
  triangle strung with cat-gut,
Or man-gut, finer than rain? It strikes the old notes,
  plucks the classical tune,
The score of seven centuries past, and on into the next
  one, the music
Ever music. I have promised you not to love the shape
  of it too well,
Or the men who touch the harp strings of their land with
  longing; promised
Not to walk Ireland's highways and by-ways without
  remembering your departure,
Not to speak the names Pearse, Connolly, McBride, or
  to mention their valor,
Not to weep my alien tears by Liffey or Shannon. I
  will look on them passing

In the turbulent current, see them in the springtime of
    what they were
And then in Dublin's winter and Athlone's, but give no
    sign. I shall hear
Their fists pounding the granite of river-walls and
    wharfs, the long dead stone,
Their faces veiled in mist, warned and bemoaned all
    autumn by the fog-horn of my heart.

2.

No questions, please. The final verdict has been
    pronounced.
Once the bones no longer boil in the heart's fluid, in that
Pot-au-feu of choicest cuts, that quivering stew, know
    that the fire
Is quenched and the catastrophe of ash is on us.
    Remnants of a better time
Is what we are, bent, tottering on the brink, gripping
    canes in our mottled claws
To hold the enemy at bay (or, better still, to crack
    his grinning skull).
"Keep your distance!" we cry out at dawn and dusk.
    You say you can't go on,
And then reverse it, and I follow the change of pace
    like the finger of a metronome,
Calling out to hungering death that there's little nourish-
    ment in us,
With even the marrow turned to dust. Instead, riding
    the gnarled hip-bones
Of skeleton nag, poor, penniless death, or tripping on
    the curve of his reaping, weeping scythe,

Consider the carrots and turnips Vladimir and Estragon
    have to offer.
These edibles, having pushed up in triumph, waving
    head-dresses of leaf and fern
In the sweet light, they alone have succulence. The
    weight of dark and damp that were their past
Is now our future, we who are plucked instant by bleak
    instant of our finery,
Stripped of our elegant feathers one by one.
But sometimes, maybe at night-fall, more likely in the
    dawn of threatening day,
When thoughts stampede in panic, hoofing and
    shouldering aside in the barricade of their corral,
Listen a while to the Hedge Row teachers and believe
    again; give eye and ear
To the poets devout among them, young as those other
    Irishmen who lean on oak or zinc
In country pubs, but the elbows of their jackets differ-
    ing. The weave of those
Who sleep on moss or stone is threadbare as spider-
    web, and no woman's needle there
To embroider the ravelling into cloth again. Or hear one
    voice keening

That long had been his wandering from far Banaloch
   to where the outlawed sages taught
In the hedges near the waters of Louch Lein; or another,
   awaking in the dew,
Saying he had walked the leather of his shoes away and
   away to reach the sound
Of the music poets spoke in the furtive, lonely lanes,
   seeking to be guided by their lore.
There were no books to open or close, no paper to set
   pen to, no pen,
Only the melody of speech running from the tongue,
   the history of learning
Fluid in the sap of the flowering hedge-row, in the silk
   of the petals,
Their names with the shudder of heartbreak in them,
   the tuition one potato a day.

3. Reincarnation

There is death in the house.
The spider trapped in the bathtub (slick as a glacier
Its polished heights) is traveler without rope, no thread
    to unwind, alone
At the end in the slipping and sliding back
Into despair. At the closed pane, the fly curses aloud.
The furtive mouse, steel necklace of trap at its throat.
Is lonelier, greyer, quieter than stone.

May not the process of return to life be so
Reversed that mouse, spider, fly, and even man,
Not having heeded the trilogy of great demands,
Be granted ever higher form until response to what is
    asked
Is acted out? ("Oh, Jonah he lived in a whale. He made
    his abode in
That fish's abdomen. Yes, Jonah he lived in a whale.")
And might not fly and spider, mouse and man
Return with the eye of the Blue Whale to offer sight
For the lone search for others of their kind; voyage

Through brine as does the Grey Whale, following
    seamarks set
Like milestones in the current, gauging the distance to
    mating
By the stars; return as Bowhead Whale, shifting ice-
    floes
As easily as scenery in the wings to make a corridor
    for those who come,
Frolicking, within his spangled wake?

So might transfigured mouse and spider, fly and man
Hear at long last the singing of the Humpback Whale,
    the arias
Of migration humming and warbling within the ancient
    flood,
And, hearing, lift on their shoulders a harpooned
    brother from the tide of blood.

4.

(on the deaths of Roger Blin
and Alan Schneider)

"Hearken," the Pawnee heralds in each stanza.
   "Hearken."
And I begin this message "hearken" so you will turn
   your head my way.
"Hearken to fervent vow and anguished prayer," the
   Pawnee says
In his own tongue, "for each god in his place grants or
   rejects man's suppliant cry."
(Hearken to the stampede of clouds called thunder as if
   it were no louder
Than the passage of dandelion hair turned white and
   drifting.)

The Pueblo knows harm is done when guests
   feast, drink and cry aloud at a funeral,
For the priest warns of the hazards if the living mourn
   over long

Or with excessive lamentation. "As the axe splinters the
   live tree," he says,
"So the ritual of the hours is sundered by grief. To weep
   while fires
Go unlit is to question the cycle of the seasons. It is
   blasphemous
To ask winter to bear guilt for its failure to be spring.
   Long bewailing,"
He says to the bereaved, "detains the spirits when they
   seek to go.
Hasten now to sprinkle the road out of the village so that
   the dust
Lies quiet under their departing feet."

At the ceremony for the dead, the priest speaks of the
   rites that lend strength
To the living who falter. "As youth departs the hearth
   for the lonely
Territory of time that lies ahead," he counsels, "so must
   the spirits
Be set free of the remembrance of the habitual trails.
   Do not ask the dead

To carry a burden of longing with them, but let them go
  with steps
As unhindered as the footfalls of spring rain. How can it
  matter
What we forget and what we remember? Memories
  belong to the living
And cannot be taken to another place. You have
  travelled along thorny ways,"
He says to the abandoned. "You have passed trees that
  have fallen in the storm,
And those you cherished are fallen among them.
  Memories wait in ambush.
Take the tumult of desolation from your ears so that the
  notes
Of bob-o-link and thrush can be heard again. Clear the
  treachery of dusk
From your eyes so that you can distinguish east from
  west, north from south.
If you go weeping through the forest, how will you find
  the way? O,
Wrench the iron of sorrow from your throats so that
  your voices are discordant no longer.

Dwell instead on the courage of the dead. They enter
   a world where they will carry
The sun as a shield and learn to use their left instead of
   their right hands."
O, hearken!

Poets

Poets, minor or major, should arrange to remain
    slender,
Cling to their skeletons, not batten
On provender, not fatten the lean spirit
In its isolated cell, its solitary chains.
The taut paunch ballooning in its network of veins
Explodes from the cumberbund. The hardening artery
    of neck
Cannot be masked by turtle-throated cashmere or
    foulard of mottled silk.

Poets, poets, use rags instead; use rags and consider
That Poe did not lie in the morgue swathed
Beyond recognition in fat. Consider on this late March
Afternoon, with violet and crocus outside, fragile as
    glass,
That the music of Marianne Moore's small polished
    bones

Was not muffled, the score not lost between thighs as
    thick as bass-fiddles
Or cat-gut muted by dropsy. Baudelaire did not throttle
    on corpulence,
Rimbaud not strangle on his own grease. In the
    unleafed trees, as I write,
Birds flicker, lighter than lace. They are the lean spirit,
Beaks asking for crumbs, their voices like reeds.

William Carlos Williams sat close, close to the table
    always, always,
Close to the typewriter keys, his body not held at bay
    by a drawbridge of flesh
Under his doctor's dress, no gangway to lower, letting
    the sauces,
The starches, the strong liquor, enter and exit
With bugles blowing. Over and over he was struck thin
By the mallet of beauty, the switchblade of sorrow,
    died slim as a gondola,
Died curved like the fine neck of a swan.

These were not gagged, strangled, outdone by the
    presence

Of banquet selves. They knew words make their way
    through navel and pore,
Move weightless as thistle, as dandelion drift,
    unencumbered.
Death happens to fatten on poets' glutted hearts.
    ("Dylan!"
Death calls, and the poet scrambles drunk and alone to
    what were once swift, bony feet,
Casting a monstrous shadow of gargantuan flesh before
    he crashes.)

Poets, remember your skeletons. In youth or dotage,
    remain as light as ashes.

On Taking up Residence in Virginia

for James Joyce

Here in this territory of state or mind, this precinct,

Bailiwick or diocese of heat and thunder-headed sky, I

Think of one who fled his native soil of church and law
and sought

A refuge between hotel rooms, afraid (as all men fear,
and fear, and fear),

Yet drew no academic robe about him, donned no skirt
of priest

Against the chill, displayed no metal emblem of his lot,
but softly walked

The cool green alien land of what had once been
diocese or bailiwick

Of home. That year, he closed the Austrian doors of
hotel rooms

(Salzburg it was) against the splintering arrows in the
sky, against

The wild black summoning of drums.

The lightning struck timber of barns, dark-eyed cattle,
    golden hay. In the applause of clouds
Colliding no sense to hark to Mozart winging from the
    Festspiele stage.
Pronged fire had ripped the harps to kindling, snapped
    the taut gut of violins;
Sweet warbling tenor, growling bass, and hearty
    baritone sang on, inaudible;
Sopranos shrieked their agony in vain.

Only when the drenched curtain of rain descended did
    his trembling cease,
And at that ending I reached out to touch the hand of
    one who now could hear,
Not music or the dying clamor of the storm, but rain,
    the Irish rain,
Come humbly to where he stood on foreign soil; the
    rain, crying
Its heart out on the Salzburg stones.

On the Death of My Student,
the Poet Serafin

Each time a perishable shadow fell
outside the office door
      room 209 Humanties Building
it was you
      the shadow is engraved there now.
The others came
      bearing the cunning subterfuge
of candle tongues that flickered an instant
haloing their greed for praise
      outlined the appetite for self
its endless scribblings on a page
      creative writing the uproarious
      name.

While you at the door
were brother to Chavez
      were and are
a bright-lipped black-crowned sultan in the vine-
   yards

reading poems to bury Marcos by
                        poems to rinse the
                        streets
of far Manila of men and women's blood
                        you reading:

      "we lived in a basement on
      divisadero street where

      my grandmother kept her
      colony of immigrants
      together with adobo and
      rice a commune of tangled tongues
      reciting rosaries to father
               flanagan on radio
               station KRAP"
reading until the hour when
the syllables of grief slipped like rain
           like tears along the wire
strung across the bay
           one dull as a cinder
among the opalescent syllables of your name
balancing sliding trembling
           from there to here.

And now the furious ego clamors
to know were the doctors expert agile enough
to scapel a poet's brow
           the ego stampedes

through the hideous massacre of Serafin
              sees his flesh
a bruised magnolia flower in the operating room
shouts out I would have entered the lancet
differently into the ivory skull! Not kept
quiet fingers on the fallen petal of his wrist
but beaten the old hawk off
              with my bare hands
broken like rattling palm fronds
the lone syllable's stiffly feathered wings
              done more
cracked the hooked beak of death
              like a blackened walnut shell!

Serafin return
I say return I cry it under the tall campus trees
there are questions I need the answers to:
how many poems were in your veins that night
and did you for a moment recognize
behind the surgeons' masks
the grinning harlequin of death's disguise
              return return
for the last long paper of the term.

One day sitting in the callous sun
you wrote a poem a joke you named "a takehome final"
              it began:

              "describe your last dream
              in your next dream"

and it ended:

> "write an obituary using
> only four and three letter
> words then
> till love
> dies cry."

Advice To the Old
(including myself)

Do not speak of yourself (for God's sake) even when
    asked.
Do not dwell on other times as different from the time
Whose air we breathe; or recall books with broken
    spines
Whose titles died with the old dreams. Do not resort
    to
An alphabet of gnarled pain, but speak of the lark's
    wing
Unbroken, still fluent as the tongue. Call out the names
    of stars
Until their metal clangs in the enormous dark. Yodel
    your way
Through fields where the dew weeps, but not you, not
    you.
Have no communion with despair; and, at the end,
Take the old fury in your empty arms, sever its veins,
And bear it fiercely, fiercely to the wild beast's lair.

Branded for Slaughter

for Shawn Wong

I have been reading, telling people I have not, knowing
    this
To be a grave illness, this searching and sorting through
    the words of others
And not ones own. I have read dark truths, such as:
    hiking over alpine paths,
Guides were struck by the scenes of massacre. No
    longer the blazing blue
Of gentianes could be found on the summits; the white
    felt clusters of stars
Called edelweiss had faded from their galaxies; the
    dwarf fern shrivelled
To dust; all that had withstood the slashing of winds, the
    onslaught of rains,
The ice of one century, the crater-hot sun in another
    season, wasted
Without outcry by the silent footprint of man.

Once cursed by the sophistry of reading, one learns
    there are places
Named My Song, My Lay, where there were other
    tramplings, assaults
Upon leaves, stems, delicate roots, small vines with
    their palms open,
Flora as delicate as the throats of the young, stalks
    snapped
Like wind-pipes. Niagara grinds the rock to mist, to
    spume, and the wasp
In autumn is parched to golden dust, writhing a little,
    then blowing,
Weightless as pollen, into the honeysuckle ditch where
    children's bodies lie.
The print of man, so vulnerable on sand, tentative on
    asphalt, shadow fallen
On the forebearing loam, is shaped like a cemetery
    stone, and on it
The names of the trampled have been inscribed.

2.

I read "collecting I traverse the garden the world," and
   recognize
The wandering poet, staff in hand, white-bearded,
   leading others
In the Adirondack dance. I read "here lilac with a
   branch of pine,"
And see pine and lilac blacken and rot, the garden the
   world stricken
Beneath the foot of poet, mountain-lover, men terrible
   in their virtue,
In the simplicity of their crime. "There is no space left
   for the footprint
Of man," is said no louder than a far plane writing its
   polluted
Mandate across the sky. Once gone, the hot mouths of
   flowers will feed
On weightless toads, humming-birds, lizards in coats of
   mail, rasping
Cicadas. Vine ropes, throbbing like arteries, will vein
   the continents
With sap; mica and quartz will glitter like planets, and
   lady-slippers

Dance again where man once tracked down the
    vegetation, as bison
Were tracked down. The paint of man stamped moss
    back into the rock;
His hand silenced great orchestras of trees, branded for
    slaughter
The lavish hills. There is no time left to summon pride
    out of the carnage,
Only the time to turn away without grieving, yes,
    without grieving,
And to go.

The Stones of a Seventeenth Century Village

Here in the South of France cicadas rasp, rasp, needles
Stuck in the grooves of August, scraping the measure
For the marching files of caterpillars, dusty accordians
Opening and closing, opening and closing in velvet
   silence
On their pilgrimage of devastation to the olive trees.

Bleached spears of wheat stand upright in the fields of
   lavender.
The stones underfoot were once pavings within the
   massive rock
Of a now vanished house. This ragged path was
   hallway
Leading from room to room. Now grass lies ashen in the
   crevices
Of broken steps that women climbed at night to the
   sound

Of children crying, grass brittle as the hair of women
Who grew old here, the strands still clinging, clawing,
Like the fingers of the drowning, to the parched scalp
    of the skull.
                    Why am I here in a strange country,
Making my way through the ruins of other women's
    houses,
Up the abandoned stairways of their soft weeping,
    while the senseless fiddling
Of the cicadas gives no warning of the advance
    of caterpillars
Through the dust toward the leaves, the trees? Is it
    because
Of the wheat stalks upright like candles in the lavender,
    that I cross
The sunken thresholds, calling too late into the
    dessication
The children's and the women's foreign names?

A Poem for Vida Hadjebi Tabrizi

A Mailgram for Babette Deutsch

As I write you, discarding for five minutes the names of
 other women and their destinies,
I dismiss as well the vengeance of distance lying
 between us, valley and tree,
Sierras and Rockies, intervening, and the salt white
 breasts of Utah
Barricades in the long drift of sand. But have we not
 called out each other's names,
And on some nights transformed the rocky myth of
 distance into a landscape
As light and shimmering as a peacock's open, quivering
 fan?
It was your poem of the gazelle standing "on legs of
 matchstick ivory,"
Your grave words saving us at last, saying that each of us
 carries in her breast

A child, holds a child there as the heart is held, anvil and
    hammer striking and striking
Through a lifetime against the bone ribs of its cage. It
    became
The child in your breast calling out to the child in mine
    across the distance,
The voice of "the passionate innocent" we had not
    instructed how to speak,
Crying out to us a total stranger's name. The voices
Of these hidden children summoned her. We had
    nothing to do with it.
Her steps were silent, as if falling on deep moss, each
    velvet spear of that carpet
Not bleached by frost as where you are, each short,
    fern-like lancet here,
Under the redwoods, hung with tears of dew; not yours,
    not mine, but tears
Of a woman who had no further use for them, a stranger
    to us, who broke the crystal string
And let them fall. You sensed her presence when you
    wrote of "immense music"
Beyond a closed and bolted door. She is the music,
    prison the bolted iron of the gate.

Her name is Vida Tabrizi. And there is more.

It comes from Iran, the fierce invocation, not by cable
  or phone call, not by letter or tongue,

But on the fugitive wind that has slipped through the
  bars. It runs, liquid as mercury,

Down the gutters of alien cities, is cried out through the
  meeting of bleeding palms

In the dark. The words of it are broken like flower
  stems between the teeth.

The message is fearful, the meaning hideously clear.

The Deciphered Message

A woman was arrested as she returned home

In the evening. But wait—not a poor woman,

Not disorderly in any way. A young woman, her hair
  black,

Teeth white, she was seen laughing on that final day.

She was well-dressed (the broad avenues of the
  residential quarter

Attest to that). She carried a brief case in her hand.

What in the world had she been up to, this woman
  arrested in Teheran?

They say French and English came easily to her tongue,
  as well as Middle Persian,
But she had been caught committing research, not on
  rocks
Or the quality of the soil, or on the lava of oil moving
  slowly,
Slow as a caravan of camels creaking across the desert
On their splayed feet. She had written about peasants,
The conditions of their days and nights. That was it.
Iranian palm trees rattled the indictment, vultures had
  the nerve
To scream it as they tore at the flesh of the living and the
  dead.
Hyenas, slope-backed in the throne room, laughed in
  high C
About it. That's how the royal family came to know.

The Geography

Tabriz is a city in Iran, home of the Blue Mosques,
Shaken by earthquakes year after year. Tabrizi is a
  woman
Who clings with finger-tips turned skeleton-white,

Clings to the edge, and we are the edge to which she
  holds,
And not quite holds, and falls, yet not quite falls,
  clinging
To our flesh and bone as though they were here own.
She is the "immense music" you wrote of behind the
  iron
Of a closed and bolted door. "Tabriz?" the curious
  ask,
Finger finding it on the map. Tabriz is a city, a place.
Tabrizi is the syllables of both our names.

This Is Not a Letter

This is not a letter

     it is not a flask of whiskey to be carried on the hip
     not wine offered across the table to you it is not
     voice of any woman speaking in complaint

(too many besides mother wife the small
   outcry of daughter have already spoken
it is now the moment for men to speak)

This is the knell of artists' voices tolling, tolling for
     one poor painter

     it is the voice of Marcel Duchamp saying

     "Make it clear as the ice of glaciers we once crossed
     together make it clear that a choice is given is
     always given

"tell him that I have been there and chose between
being the broken handle of a man or the skeleton
of a painter all the bones in place

"tell him I said a choice is offered but not for long
not like a bargain-sale when summer turns to win-
ter this choice is offered maybe once and it is now
his hour of decision forty years old the time of
man's despair

"tell him Wols is a handful of chipped marble shat-
tering the windshield of a cop's car that Wols is a
ripped canvas that can't be painted over that lies
forgotten at the back exit tell him there is a front
door to walk through if he can see it stumbling
drunken in the dark"

This is not a letter
      it is the tolling of voices it is John von Wicht saying

"I have told him if his hand the precision of it is any-
thing to him if his brain so quick has ears to listen
with then he must listen

"tell him I have cried tears for him in my bed at night
cried for the two men the wrong one the right one

tell him I have cried and now I cannot cry any-
more for him it makes me sick it breaks my heart"

And now it is Wols's voice shouting from his tor-
mented grave into the silence
                    "Ne te detruis pas, imbecile!"

It is Wols's voice
    choked with the dirt of France burned dry by *mille
    e tre* quarts of lava molten in his blood
                                        saying

"do not tear the curtains from the windows do not
puke your heart onto the cobbles and grind it to
leather under your black heel do not rock your-
self in your arms for solace whispering this is one
night only there will be others to retrieve it *ce n'est
pas vrai! ce soir est tous les soirs!* each night you
rage with is one more passage in a honeycomb of
foul decay *je te le dis* women fight over my re-
mains counterfeit pencil gouache oil to sell as mine
and I? I am lonely here in the dark take my place
for an hour *seulement une heure pour que je puisse
chauffer mon coeur au soleil de la vie.*"

What Parents Do Not Yet Know

The tree that lingers at the window is just sixteen,
And you, uneasy parent of its wanton ways,
Eavesdrop upon the whispering of three-fingered
    leaves.

The pale pink squirrel who dances in the nude,
Chattering of nuts, with eyes that see five ways,
Is not related to the tree's anomalies, nor grieves

That you, tormented guardian of bark and roots
And leaves, must seek for words to ratify the pact.
You were once witness to departing wings that fled
    defiantly

One winter night; hear now the fragile music as it
    weaves
Like ivy through the cawing of the crows. Not wasp,
    or cattle ant, or bee

Is hesitant, for each believes his paragon of industry
   is what
Transforms a tree to child, and child to tree again
   (with softly whispering leaves).

A Poem for the
Students of Greece

On the weekend, the upholstery of a sofa was re-
    placed
In the lobby, the gracious lobby of the Acropole
    Palace Hotel.
A student carried there at dawn had bled to death,
Had bled to death on the brocade. By noon in the
    lobby,
The classical lobby, where magazines are sold, the
    marble floor
Had been scrubbed clean of any trace, of any trace.
    In the lobby
Imported perfumes and foreign papers may be
    bought, and by noon
The marble was scrubbed clean of the reflection
    of the dying student's
Face. Athenians and tourists spent the evening at
The usual night-clubs, the customary places, saying -

Saying what?
When street-lights hang by swinging wires
And voices in the dark cry, "Thailand, Thailand,"

What can be spoken of in night-clubs,
In the customary places? When voices
Unacquainted yet with terror call
Their summons from the barricades,
"Parents, join us! We are your children!
We fight the battle for you! Do not let us die!"
What answers can be given in the customary
Places, in the desecrated lobby
Where a student bled to death on the brocade?

"I took life, and faced her," Neruda answers gently;
"And won her, and then went through
The tunnel of the mines
To see how other men live . . .
When I came out, my hands stained
With garbage and sadness, I held
My hands up and showed them to the generals,
And said: 'I am not a part of this crime.'"

We have been told many things, many things,
By the wise, by those who read deeply, deeply in
   books,
And, reading, perhaps miss the sudden, wild pass-
   age of wings
At dusk, miss the white lanterns of magnolia lit on
   the branch,
The tapers of Bishop Pine trembling before the altar
   of night,

Miss the blazing of winter cones split open by dawn,
    and the green,
The unfading green of the olive under its canopy of
    leaves.
The wise have said poetry explores the landscape
    of the self,
And the defiant ask if that isolate and lonely territory
    cannot be
Blighted by drought, without oasis, its single well,
    its single tree
No more than mirage. The defiant say
The voice that cries "I, I" is dry as a locust's rasping
    wing.
We are told by those who read deeply, deeply, into
    books
That time for a poet is a metronome pacing the gait
Of his heart, that uncertain gait, while time
For the writer of prose is a clock hanging on the wall
    of his century; or told
That prose is a Coney Island mirror, poetry a win-
    dow through which
Man seeks to see beyond the glass.

                    How does one deal with suppositions
                    such as these?

Nanon, Maskaleris, where are the words, whether
    poetry

Or prose, to speak of the Acropole Palace windows
    facing
The university's green iron gate that hangs twisted
    on its hinges
After what took place? Is there poetry or prose in
    any tongue
To say that on the weekend the upholstery of a sofa
    was replaced
In the lobby where foreign newspapers are sold, to
    say
By noon of that first day the marble floor was
    scrubbed clean of any trace?

    "I am thinking of that age to come," Henry Miller
    Wrote for those who have closed their windows,
       their doors,
    "When men will fight and kill for God . . . when
       food
    Will be forgotten . . . I am thinking of a world
    Of men and women with dynamos between their
       legs,
    A world of natural fury, passion, action, drama,
       madness, dreams . . ."

What role is left to us, what choice? What words
Can we take in our hands to give the shape of bricks,
    to shape to bricks,
Such as those clawed from the walls of places where
    learning

Is barricaded; what color the bricks, the vocabulary
   flung
At tanks, at helmets, into wave after ripping wave
   of gas
That twists tears from the eyes, wrings eyes from
   the head?
Now that the bricks are gathered in shallow piles,
   become
Monuments marking the graves of the young, how
   can we say again,
   In what language: "On the weekend, the upholstery
   of a sofa
In the lobby was replaced, and the marble floor
   scrubbed clean
Of any trace"?

   There are men who seek to look
   Through the window of a poem of their own mak-
    ing,
   Gaze raptly there until the glass clouds with their
    breath,
   Leaving only the inner landscape of despair. Lew
    Welch was one who,
   Before shattering the pane, turned back from death
    to say:

      "Poets carry the news, they warn the
       prince,"
      And asked of us who could not answer:

"Has nobody said out loud
Our job is to give ourselves away? That
Now and then we must rest from that work?
That this is the resting-place?"

Ritzoes, poet of Greece, poet of prison, poet of house
    arrest,
Answers the questions about the sofa, the lobby,
    about the clock,
The metronome, answers Lew's question about rest-
    ing from the job,
Answers the tanks, the tear-gas, the young dead,
    saying:

"They sit transfixed high in their outposts
. . . scanning the tormented ocean
Where the broken mast of the moon has sunk.
They have run out of bread, exhausted their muni-
    tions.
Now they load their cannons with their hearts.
So many years beseiged by land and sea
They have starved, they have been slaughtered,
Yet none has perished.
High in their outposts their eyes shine . . ."

(SALONIKA and Athens 1973)
(Revised November 20, 1975)

A Poem for the Teesto Diné
of Arizona

The mountain is old. They say she is a female moun-
tain.
The women who know her are not young, yet they
call her
The Mother. She stands tall against the sky, fragrant
with herbs,
Embellished by shrubs. The mantle that falls from
her shoulders
Changes color, tree-shadow by shadow, as it drifts
to the valley,
Changes texture in slope after slope of grain. Her
earrings
And rings are shrines for the healing ceremonies.
Offerings
Of turquoise, abalone, jet, coral and white shells are
brought

To her now, as in other centuries, gifts for the Holy
    People
Who live in her veins. She is The Mother who stands
    in silence
When the land is fettered and barbed with wire,
    when it is parched
To dust by the drought of uniformed men.

    (Take a look at Mr. Relocation
    As he comes dancing, prancing
    Up the pike, cha-cha-ing to the music
    Of hidden coal in the Mesa, comes hushing
    The blare of the bugles of uranium, finger
    On lips, duet of handcuffs at his belt keeping time
    With the intricate steps of his macabre dance.)

What can be said, or written, or cried out to Roberta
    Blackgoat,
To Ruth Bennally, to Pauline Whitesinger, whose lives
Have been lived at Big Mountain, who graze their
    cattle there?
"When the time comes, if we don't have any choice,"
    is what Ruth Bennally is saying,

"We'll fight with our fists." They have seen the tres-
    passers come
To garrote the ceremonial hogans, dynamite the
    sacred springs.
"When I fired," is what Katherine Smith says, "they
    were fencing
Right across the wash from my home. Indian police
    came to arrest me.
I told them they couldn't. They were my sons, the
    same blood
Was running in our veins. Only a white man can ar-
    rest me, was
What I told them. So the white men came and took
    me away."
And Pauline Whitesinger whispers: "They can shoot
    me standing here
In my bare feet. I won't put shoes on for them," her
    voice
Quiet as the foot-fall of a deer.

    ("Relocation" is the word, the death sentence given
    To people with another look in their eyes,
    To those with the beaks of eagles, who carry
    Their history with them as they go. It is a word

For the uprooting of trees, for the turning to stone
Of sap under city streets, for the harnessing
Of deep rivers in a ravished land.)

In Flagstaff, prayers cannot be offered to Big Moun-
tain.
In Flagstaff, the medals and uniforms speak of other
things.
But far in the dark, thunder shouts down the long
impounding:
Impounding of the singular music of ore in the hills,
Impounding of the slumber of coal, impounding,
impounding;
Far in the dark, trees grieve aloud in the wind,
Bemoaning the long enduring of the Cherokees'
Trail of Tears,
The Navajos' Long Walk of their despair. In the
dark,
Horns of lightning rip wide the night. Oh, believe
me, believe me,
There will be more in the end than the labyrinths of
rusted wire
And the empty tear-gas cannisters left on the tram-
pled grass.

Poem for a Painter Bent
on Suicide

You drive a hard-nosed, ungelded bargain
With the times. You demand the last penny
Be paid in full, even though broken like a heart
Or colt. Can you accept this fiscal year
As a loan I offer (at exorbitant interest),
To be repaid over the legal interim required
For cancelling death? (Or will you choose
To slash with the artist's savage brush "no funds"
Across the canvas of your self-portrait's face?)

Is there a music in the means men take
To file their bankruptcies? Is it done
In any tongue as modest as poetry is,
That *compte rendu* in which the deficit to leap,
Or hang, or sever is written savagely in red?

This autumn accept the last half of April,
Deposited to your account in perpetual
Annuity, the balance to be paid in green-backed
Summer days and currency of nights in silver change.
All this to be kept in safe deposit tins within a vault,
Beneath the tick-tacking of the hearts of lonely men
Who feared not auditor or poetry's devaluation
When they chose to die, but something less:
The forgery of their embezzled faces in a shattered
   glass.

A Poem for February
First 1975

for Jessica Mitford

Glance back four years (yes, nearly four years now,
No matter how close, how shuddering the grief).
  Glance back
To the bonfires, to the curve of the moon lighting
  the walkways, the catwalks,
Lighting the faces of those who stood, arms locked,
  black links of a chain
Twisting motionless through D-Yard, a barrier of
  men, alive still
But rigid as the dead. That September the white
  horns of the moon and the bonfires
Shone for a moment in the lonely caverns of their
  eyes.

Hear the far clang of the syllables: Attica. Do not
  let them

58

Slip through the crevices of history, geography, be
    effaced from
The miraculous ledger of the stars. Say that a civiliza-
    tion was lost here,
Near to a city named for a dying species, Buffalo,
    not in that other Attica
Leafed delicately with quivering olive trees, washed
    on two sides by the Aegean Sea,
A triangle of ancient Greece refreshed by small,
    blue, brimming harbors,
Touched gently by the south wind as it passed. The
    heights were
Violet-crowned, the fields sweet with jasmine, the
    townships
Of ancient Attica bore the names of various plants
    and trees.
Its people are said to have walked gracefully through
    the luminous
Ether of its dusks. (Why not, with no irons at their
    ankles, no shackles
At their wrists?) That Attica overlooked the plain
    of Marathon,
Descended rock by sunbleached rock to the bright
    pulsing sea.

Do these things matter now?

The men locked arm in arm in the Attica of our dust,
     our maggots, our dereliction, stand
Halted at the edge, high on their hushed precipice,
     men whose names we have since learned,
Who choked, who wept, who fell on their knees in
     D-Yard as the helicopter dipped
And let its cargo of gas drift, lazy as smoke, quiet as
     cloud formations,
Across the rainy dawn. It is said that in ancient Attica
Torch-light processions descended from Athens,
     rejoicing, and turned the coastline
Radiant, fanned the dark harbors into waltzing light.
     What torches can we carry,
Lit by the dry kindling of our hearts?

At the first burst of rifle fire, those whose stark names
     we have since learned
Were mowed down like grain, their blood darker than
     poppies lying, dying,
In the wheat, and the single curse, "Rockefeller," cut
     deep in the curve of each bullet

That scythed them down. Down, down the walkways
    the assault units
Advanced in their curtain of fire, their cloaks of flame,
    came in yellow rain-gear,
In beetle-eyed masks, elephant-nosed, without ears, so
    that the pounding
On doors was silence to them, the pounding of fists at
    humble doors where
The locks broke, the wood split wide to the knocking,
    the knuckles of lost men
Beating at Rockefeller's door, inmates, hostages,
    pounding all night,
Pounding into the dawn like taps sounding at the barrier
    of his grinning door.
'If he had come, showed that he cared,' whispered the
    ashes of the extinguished fires,
'Things would have been different. Men would have
    lived who had not asked to die.'

As one approached ancient Attica, it is said that a
    change of temperature
Could be perceived, a softening of the breath of the
    wind, of the wash of the sea.

That Attica was famed for its marble (not for its blood),
   marble astonishingly white,
Astonishingly blue; famed as well for the brittle
   charcoal of its fuel.
(Charcoal obtained from bones is called 'bone black' in
   the trade.
It lay on the pavings of D-Yard after the fires were done
   and the pounding ceased on the stone
Of one man's door.) 'If he had come it would have
   shown . . .' whispered the blowing ash.
But does not stone hold echoes in the hollow of its
   hands, echoes
That call forever down the corridor of history, across
   the congregation of the years,
Calling that all we can know of our own lives is learned
Through the despair of men whose names are not our
   own?
Remember the word Attica. Remember its syllables
   clanging, clanging.
Do not let them go.

After the Earth Quaked

to the memory of
Emanuel Carnevali

After the earthquake, a phenomenon of quiet
Spread, avocado-green, across the land,
The voices of trees still hushed
By the upbraiding of the dark earth's shuddering.
Birds had taken it well; pictures were straightened
In houses; no cracks veined the walls,
No garden gate hung unhinged by
The disturbed slumber of the daffodils; all this
Under the untroubled gaze of distant planets
And lesser stars. The Italian poet, Carnevali,
Once wrote: "The earthquake has little fingers.
You can find the truth in this
In the falling of tiny bits of plaster from the walls."

This morning, he would have written in the reign of
  quiet
That the earthquake was God clenching his trembling
  fist

63

To threaten man on the highways and by-ways of all he
    had
Become. He would have set it down again: "Hesitating
Everywhere, hesitating fearfully, the few poets, they
    who weigh
With delicate hands, walk on the unfrequented roads,
Meandering, crying and laughing against the rest."

To a Proud Old Woman
Watching the Tearing Down
of the Hurricane Shed

You did not see wood blackened by rot, or
    rust-emblazoned iron,
Or gutter riddled like a cabbage leaf. No, none of these.
Not jagged flower-pot, tile without echo, table without
    leg, or chair bereft
Of arms, or planks stiped with mildew like a zerba's
    hide.
Each board they fed the flame, bepearled with slug,
    viscous
With writhing worm, remained for you bleached
    timber of another year,
Crowned with lacy green, forever tree, within the static
    of your memory.

But there in the old shed's dying your youth died,
    mourned only
By the turtle-doves this spring. The child and girl
    and woman named Felicity
Watched by the strong sea-wall in separate agonies;
    the breasts, limbs, lovely cranium of all you were

Consumed at last, and through clenched teeth you
    cried your hideous name.
Yours were the entrails twisting in the flame, the life
    of all you were to be
Dragged, screaming, from the shed's long dying,
    ash now with the poems not written,
Grace not said, blowing at evening to the dead-end
    of the driveway's ending.
This was a devastating of the past you could not
    countenance. It brought you to your knees
That night under the pale tears of the dogwood's
drifting leaves.

But there have been other executions, fiercer, bloodier.
    There have been
More savage dramas played, when the rope of terror
    tightened on the throat
And the neck jerked, broken like the heart, your hand
    nor any other lifted, and no requiem sung.
Think of these others now that the last, radiant embers
    of the shed are dust.
Not for long does the high wind of life take words we
    speak
From out our mouths, and bear them swiftly, clearly
    through the air
So that the living and the murdered dead may hear.

(Let it be courage that our tongues compose,
There being no refuge from the hurricane that blows.)